Pieces of a
Tormented Mind

Pieces of a Tormented Mind

Antara Banerjee

HAWAKAL

HAWAKAL

Published by Hawakal Publishers
185 Kali Temple Road, Nimta, Kolkata 700049
India

Email info@hawakal.com
Website www.hawakal.com

First edition October, 2019

Cover design: Antara Banerjee

ISBN: 978-93-87883-81-9

Price: 350 INR | USD 11.99

to *my Mother*,
my pillar of support, my most severe critic,
my closest confidante...
She, who taught me to be stubborn, to be
strong, to be bold.

FOREWORD

It has been a very moving and emotional experience for me, to go through this exceptionally powerful and articulate book of poems by Antara.

Antara's artistic and liberating poems are untamed, uninhibited and brutally honest. The facile way she strings her words and ideas to create extraordinary images, reaches out to touch the soul. It is a mastery we rarely come across in contemporary Indian poetry.

She has a magical and mesmerising way with words, technique and method. The manner in which she deals with subjects like nature, romance, emotions, feminism, cruelty and such, is enhanced by her ability to create a greatness with words that resonate with rhythm and ideas.

As I see, the book is divided into two sections, *Romantic* and *Rebel*, which essentially explore the two facets of the poet.

In *Romantic*, Antara has embraced the theme of conditional and unconditional love in a rather extraordinary way, and I dare say, with great honesty. 'Love' is a word we use very nonchalantly these days, however, defining it is hard. But, not for this poet! She has written about it with great finesse, delving into the pleasure, the pain, the rejection while also exploring the sensual and sexual aspect of it.

Pleasure and pain have been beautifully explored in poems like, "On the Edge," "Price," "Mine," and others. The poem, "Fragrances that Linger," beautifully evokes a great sense of nostalgia for pleasures experienced in the past. It stirs memories in us, of that special perfume, that special fragrance of someone's body that lingers on. While reading, "When I am Silent," I was filled with awe and wonder, at the unveiling of the myriad ways in which silence speaks to us. In the "Arachnid Conspiracy," she has brilliantly described the process of life using a spider's web as a metaphor, as to how beauty can be deceitful and lethal.

In the second section, *Rebel*, Antara, strongly and unabashedly lashes out at the pummelling of innocents by those in power, at bought media, our cruelty towards animals and humans alike. "I Refuse," is the poet's take on what is going utterly wrong with today's world. Its emotional quotient hits you exactly where it is meant to hurt.

She champions the cause of women in an extraordinarily powerful poem, "Change." The last lines of the poem say it all:

"Stand up woman! Wear your crown
There's much more in store,
Live your life in honour and glory
It's worth dying for!"

I hope Antara continues her artistically exhilarating work, so that her readers may continue to enjoy the immense pleasure of reading her.

Mahabanoo Mody-Kotwal

Author's Note

If prose is a piece of life, verse is the voice of the soul.

I do not know if poetry can ever be taught or learnt...or if one should even try.

It is the primordial yearning of the soul to gush out in love or to scream out in pain...to harden as a rebel or to melt into a romantic mush. No wonder, poetry appeared even before man had begun to write. Verse, therefore, is the song of the soul.

Poetry can express mirth, distress, anger, amour, erotica, pain or for that matter any emotion with a lyrical intensity that nothing else can bring forth.

There is a saying: *A picture speaks a thousand words* but I have always believed that the imagination that exquisitely carved words can evoke, far exceeds any vision the human eyes can witness...because, imagination is bound by nothing.

Please do not read my poetry in my context, the beauty of words comes alive only when it is read as one's own...as the voice of one's own soul and one's own experiences...I mean not to express my emotions but to evoke yours with my words.

Antara Banerjee

CONTENTS

Romantic

Rebel

ROMANTIC

On the Edge

Romance must always live on the edge.
Revel in life, at the brink of death.
Teeter unsure, knowing all the while,
the world could end, but love wouldn't die.
Look into the mirror, laugh at the witch,
To endear and yet, stay out of reach.
To follow the heart, not think and leap,
be cursed by a fairy, to an endless sleep.
Sigh in sorrow, sob in pain,
burn in the sun and drench in rain.
To have nothing, yet want to give,
dream of Helen, launch a thousand ship.
Prepare to go, when you want to stay,
to feign indifference, and walk away.
To drink elixir, from Lucifer's peg,
a broken heart, not much at stake.
Hire yourself to Mephistopheles,
damn the soul, to hell on lease.
Become a beggar, beg for love,
renounce Solomon's own treasure trove.
Join the Norse Gods, in the Great Hall feast,
elope with beauty, irk the beast.
Commit the sins, suffer like a fool,

become a hermit, go back to school.
To hit the bottom, reach the peak,
to narrate an epic, then never speak.
Blow caution to the wind, open Pandora's box,
Romance is after all, a charming paradox.

Thousand & One Nights

Sleep not my love, keep awake
through a
Thousand and One Nights.
Look into my eyes...
I have abandoned sleep forever.
Promise! You shall lock me
into your handsome wakefulness,
for eternity...

Let me conjure wondrous tales,
let not the stream of visions abate,
for I know,
the merciless scimitar awaits
the end of the legend...

I shall meet your dare,
keep up the stories.
Death scares me not,
but this swaying is delicious...
the end... or the legend
through a
Thousand and One Nights...

The eerie music of the desert
plays on the serpentine ripples
of the undulating dunes.
Lilting to the tunes,
adders dance sideways.
The moon descends quietly
on the silver domes
and the scorpions rejoice!

Bottle the djinns,
for there is not a wish
left unfulfilled.
Let the kalandars
whirl into a white haze.
Let the midgets
lick obscene pleasures
into the pink clefts
of the white houris.
Let the black slave roll
on the silken rug
fornicating the favourite queen...
Let the white stallions
rip through the lush forests
while the forty thieves
raid the heavens tonight!
Open sesame!
Let the curtains be flung open
Let God close his eyes...
as we remain locked
in this unsleeping bliss forever
forever...
through the
Thousand and One Nights....

Naive Bard

What allure draws you
to the wrong goddess,
O, naive bard!
You plead death,
while I desire
to grant you a boon!

You bathe me
not in blood,
but a deep blue potion,
or is it venom?!

Remember?
You always sought
to taste the lethal fluid?

You promised-
'I shall unveil the secret
with my life...
and whisper
the taste to you,
even as I lay dying...
You! Only you,

shall know!
Unless it robs my memory
of this promise.'

I say,
'Poison brings death
not forgetfulness!
O naive bard!
That taste
shall carry over
to your afterlife...
remain coiled
in the memory of your tongue,
forever...
So be it!
I consign you
to reptilia!
Forked tongue, poison fangs
scaled skin...'

'Be born
of a serpent's womb!'

'Welcome death!
Join the venomous clan!
Drown the world
in your lethal intoxication!'

You, have been blessed!

Fragrances that Linger

A creeper
of fragrant wild wisteria
winds around my body.
The tender green foliage
covers my skin.
The cascading blooms
hang in abundance,
dancing and lilting
in the rousing wind.
Purple and pink blossoms
bloom at the dimple of my navel...

The scent travels with me,
pervading the air...
like a drop of warm rouge
dissolving in a swirl of water...
Drink from the goblet of amour,
when you pass by me...
This is a fragrance
that shall linger.

I shall take root in your heart,
grow on your soul...

bathe in your desires...
drown you in delicacy...

I am invasive...
I shall persist...
Love me... be mine...
dwell in me...
Forever!

When I am Silent

When you hear nothing from me...
when I am silent.
When no poetry seems to flow
in the air around you,
know, that I am still around...

Know, that I am fighting my body
spinning out of control...
aching to be touched.
Wetting my lips...
parched from not meeting yours for long...
Hiding the red streaks in my eyes...
rubbing my skin,
to conjure your fragrance...
that, which might be leftover
from your last touch.

When no poetry seems to flow
in the air around you...
know, that I am still around,
for this silence is a desperate attempt
to prevent gushing over... to prevent
flooding you with my private emotions.

Though, they can hardly be called
private anymore...
They are all, about you...

But sometimes,
the floodgates need to be closed,
lest the exceeding love,
the swollen emotions, overflow...

I let myself go... I turn to silence...

Know that when no poetry
is flowing around you...
I am still there.
More intense than ever,
more turbulent,
more encompassing...
more present...
when I am silent.

Monsoon

This season of wanton abundance,
when the sensually yielding clouds
pour for no reason at all...
When the vapoured mist
veiling the window panes
sends mischievous messages
to the curious passersby...
Wonder, what steamy shadows
might be stirring inside.

The cuckoo goes on pleading deliriously,
'Love me... love me do!'

Wet orchards drip the nectar
of overripe fruits.
The fallen flowers breathe
irresistible fragrances into the air.
The drenched leaves bend over,
in coy submission,
and the rains pour...

The sun...
the moon... the stars...

hide behind the thick nimbus clouds...
lest the streaks of amorous want
show on their bashful countenance.
Days blur into hazy dusks...
Nights into mushy dawns...
like the inseparably mingled bodies
of two crazed lovers.

A strange hunger
benumbs the body,
a disturbing tautness tugs at the limbs...
it demands a forbidden cure...
Who shall quell this fire?
This unbearable pricking of thorns all over...
This sweet venom
flowing in the veins,
yearns for a potent nostrum...

Arachnid Conspiracy

It swung innocently
in the morning breeze,
a cozy hammock
of diamond dewdrop strings.
Reflecting the colours of rainbow,
as the sun touched it
in the misty, dreamy dawn.
A fine filigree lace
of pristine white silk,
invisible almost
till I ventured too close.

Who knew of the
arachnid conspiracy,
until I walked
into the innocuous web?

Tangly spirals
of inseparable mesh
reinforced with
spittle glue.
It swirled around me,
winding me
in its lethal web,
A silk trap

of sure death!

Now, it appeared,
the gluttonous fiend!
The evil eyes
of the ruthless arachnid,
Waiting smugly
in a distant corner,
savouring my agony
with obscene delight.

Each attempt to escape,
closed the trap
tighter still.
The diamond dew drops fell away,
the white lace turned into
the tangly grey hair
of a haggard witch.

I was trapped,
into a treacherous snare,
of a hopeless and
despondent terror.
Death came crawling
on all eight,
and weighed me down
with its crushing heft.

Life has indeed been
a deceitful arachnid,
snaring me into a death trap
killing me
with those
tangly, treacherous
alluring dreams!

Half Truths

Who is this 'you'
that appears in my poetry so often?
Is it really you?
Or someone I imagine,
in your guise...
Or is it a stranger,
to whom I write
in such earnest passion?

This 'you',
whom I desire..love... invoke...
Is it really you?
My hands tremor
with a benumbing amour,
lips tremble,
as each word
passes through the fervent quill.
They spread themselves abundant,
on the inviting chest of the papyrus,
reveal themselves
to the gaze of the hungry reader.

There are no answers, still...
It is a shadowy trail...
Sometimes it is you...
you, and no one else.
Sometimes, a shadow
of someone like you...
a masked impostor...
a rogue indeed!

Ask me not, to swear by anything,
Poets are prone to liberties,
you know?
Alternate reality...
A parallel universe...
They are easily led astray,
they lead astray too...
for they remain in denial forever.
Never admit,
that they live in half truths!

Immortal Beloved

No one can invest everything in love,
as a true artist can.
No one can be as passionate.
Immortal is that love,
for it goes beyond the limits of reason
and sanity...
Where attachment becomes eccentric,
crushing love, guises as disdain...
being and not being, mingle into one...
a state of eternal thirst.

Pain becomes inspiration,
a zeal, in which an entire life
can be dedicated....
in the quest of a drop
of that ever-elusive fulfilment...

It indeed takes
a weaver of dreams
to make an immortal beloved
out of a mortal love...

Price

I ground myself to dust,
in the crushing mill
of unrelenting love.
Blew myself to wind,
in your quest.
I trusted like a child,
entrusting itself to life...
Waited as though
death would never come...

I broke the goblet
of my brimming heart
many times over...
Slashed my dreams
to keep awake for you...
Whispered your name
into the ears of the wind...
Called out to you
at the dead of my sleepless night...

What did you do, my love?
What price did you pay?

Mine

Why must a day pass
without the hope of seeing you?
Without the tingle of your voice
in my ears?

It is not easy to wring mead
out of mere memories...
to quench the thirst of a parched heart.
Restless days blur into sleepless nights,
they hang around in the darkness,
drowned in a haze of tears...

Yes, I cry for you...
But tell me why,
I must lay my soul bare,
to beget
what I know, is mine?

I Knew

I knew it was you...
when I did not know you at all...
is this called destiny?

Did you not feel it too?
A sudden glow that lighted up?
The moment when the mundane
turned extraordinary!

What was that secret that reflected
from your eyes into mine,
and warmed my heart to the core?
How does this happen?
What does it mean?
How much time does it take
to know your own from the rest?

Fie!
Only the blind and foolish
ask such questions.

Hopelessly in Love

How can someone be
hopelessly in love?
Isn't there always a hope
for reciprocation?
A possibility
to be loved as dearly too?
An assurance
that someone will be there...
forever...
waiting as eagerly to touch...
to embrace...
to be embraced...
to be one
and the only one...
when ever, where ever,
whichever way...

Hopelessly in love,
is not so hopeless after all...

Sleepless Night

Even as I struggle
to find sleep
at the cusp of the night
and the dawn.
She eludes me stubbornly...

A pair of tormented eyes
haunt me instead.
Those, which struggled too.
Those sure feet
that struggled against walking away.
A throbbing silence,
to hold back something
that would perhaps
never be told.
But that,
which the heart
shall always return to.

A few magic moments
stolen from life...
an unknown tale
within the sudden recesses

of the known one.
Verses...melodies...intimacies
from another world...
another time...

Who says,
words speak the universe?
I am sure,
Silence does!

The Fall

I felt like a wizard,
when my words
stirred you from a distance.
I enamoured
in defying the laws of gravity.
That, I could fly to you
at will...

But who knew
that bliss
would be so short lived?
That, like Icarus,
waylaid by hubris,
I would fly
too close to the sun
And fall!
Fall...
spinning helplessly
into the sea of Agean.

Never to surface again!
Never to dare!
Never soar in the sky!
Never to return to my words-
to stir you again!

Unsung

Something is broken somewhere,
like the string
of a melancholy song.
The muffled melody
flows no more.
Let the silence prevail,
for there was never an audience.
No one misses
an unheard symphony
A mute song, with garbled lyrics
goes unsung...

Something is torn somewhere,
like the cord of a half woven dream...
The loom doesn't accept new yarn,
It refuses to be knotted too.
Abandon the half baked vision,
beautiful though it may have been,
for no eyes desire it anymore,
no sleep permits its passage....

Something is dashed somewhere,
a fledgling in flight...

Unsure new wings,
that couldn't stand the storm.
Leave the fledgling alone,
for it is beyond redemption now.
It had sinned to hope for a flight,
And now it lies askew on the ground,
beside the debris of its broken nest.

Something is dead somewhere,
like the corpse
of an unidentified unknown...
No one claims the remains.
Let it be run over,
again... and again... and again...
Let it flatten to the ground
not only in body...
but also in spirit,
Let the story end
without a funeral.
A nameless death,
without the hope
of an afterlife ever.

Nothing and Nought

Laughters have lost their sheen,
the chest numb,
I feel the painful
unfeeling of pain.
Lost is the hope of
your return too.

Yet, my breath stifles
at the thought of growing apart,
for complicated equations
still persist between us....
Though they all
add up to a 'Nought' now.
They have inhabited
our mathematics for long
and they still dwell
in our books.

I now realize,
'Nothing' and 'Nought'
are not the same...
There is a sea of difference
between them...

The 'Nought' cannot be ignored,
cannot be erased
out of the past and the present.
It is not vacuum!
Invisible life forms dwell
in its seemingly empty sphere.
The death of 'Nought'
is tragic, no less!

Then, how am I to let go?
Discard the arithmetic
of laughter and mirth,
misgivings and hurt?
Tear off the pages
full of our trials and errors?
Our desperate attempts
to balance it all again.

Remember the stick diagrams
we used to draw together?
They still stand holding hands,
amidst the crowd of scribbles.
But now,
they have grown stiff,
awkward and estranged.
It is hard to go back to those pages
for they turn to dust
when I try to revisit them...
The horror of 'Nothing'
follows the 'Nought'.

So, I reconcile the book of accounts
with fake contras

and collect the 'Noughts'
in a wicker basket too!

But every time
the unwieldy 'Noughts'
spill out and I lose them...
filling me with the terror
of the imminent
'Nothing'!

In Words

I live in words,
I need words to survive...
It's important to know,
if the letters still gel,
if they still hold hands...
make music together.
If they still
yearn for one another.

I live in words,
that hang from my windows
like wind chimes.
Stirred by the slightest hint of breeze,
I survive in that melody.

In words, I live,
that flow from my pen...
filled with the colour of your love,
create poetry... make the heart ache...
I survive in those verses.

I live in words,
for they span distances,

speak for me, for you
and all that would
remain unspoken otherwise.
I gather the world around me
within my words,
I survive in the crystal palace
of my poetry,
with the words that consist
a kingdom of my own.

Beyond Betrayal

Last night,
of all nights,
was the perfect occasion,
for a night long call.
But to leave you
with my thoughts
seemed the best way
to be with you.

I spoke your name
to my pillow,
perhaps a million times...
heart aflutter with your thoughts
skin sore with want.
My body
awash with your fragrance...
In the darkness
you lingered with me...
till a dreamless sleep
did us apart.

I brushed up
on my 'past participles' today.

'Broken heart'
came up as a verb,
'a verb, that is an adjective'.

Maybe, it is not uncommon
to be in shambles;
to become an adjective
to someone's verb.
To be betrayed,
to have every emotion
knocked down
till the heart descends
into a stony numbness.

I had reconciled with that too,
till you walked out of a sweet memory
and gathered me in your arms,
as though rescuing a rag doll...
Made love to me
like a God,
carried me to heaven and
breathed life into me once more...

That moment
of infinite fulfilment
had come
and is over.
But you left me throbbing again,
erasing my way back
to that familiar numbness.
It hurts now...
it really does!

No, I am not looking to
mend my broken heart.
And I know,
I cannot mend yours either.
But there is a hope
that this would save
a greater dissipation...
with something
greater than love perhaps,
-something,
that would survive,
like a resuscitated heart
-something,
beyond betrayal...

Rendezvous

The furies
are pouring down
on earth tonight...
the awesome symphony
of the clouds
and the rains,
is reverberating
around the dark firmament.
Thunderous applauses
are clapping across the skies
as lightning cleaves
the doors of the prudish heaven.
The oceans surge
with crazed waves,
lashing out on the shores.
The tortured rocks
shatter and crumble
into the turbulent waters helplessly...
See
what was fated for you and me tonight!
We were destined to be swept away!
to drown in a deluge,
to die a fluid death!

To be washed
to the shores of another world...
to another dream...
It's a pity,
we failed to keep the rendezvous
Lost the magnificent moment!
Why death?
you ask....
Don't you see?
Some deaths are
more precious than life...
sweeter than several lifetimes...
Those that would endure...
only if we had the heart...
had courage enough,
to meet them!

Farewell

It is strange
how mirth translates into pain...
as the drums
beat the mind
into an intoxicating trance.
The dear one, is leaving tonight,
drawing the festivities
to a poignant close.

My eyes grow moist,
at the parting rituals...
the smear of red vermillion,
on golden cheeks...
the crazed dancers,
swirling to a mad rhythm....
the piercing ululations
of the women in red...

Yet I trace a cast down look
on the beloved's face.
Ah ache...heart ache
burning the eyes!

The countenance of the clay god
looks morose.

To bid farewell is hard...
to be bidden farewell is not easy too!
Sweets, betel leaf,
the vermillion haze and tears...
There she goes...
sinking slowly into the water...
her descent,
to the other side.

It would take
another year of grinding wait,
till joy returns.
But it also gives a reason to hope
for another time of togetherness,
To be away from the beloved
and yet
keep faith...

Farewell beloved!
You shall be awaited...
in eager anticipation...
in love... in pain...

REBEL

Pieces of a Tormented Mind

I auctioned out
my soul today,
sold my silence
to the highest bid.

The cantankerous gold
tinkles in my pocket...
But it's jingle breaks my heart.
For now,
I am a beggar,
with a tainted soul.

The silenced words rebel
within the walls
of my tormented mind.
It's a shame that
my silence makes music,
in someone else's song.

I curse you
for this humiliation,
you have forced
down my throat.
You have silenced my words...

those that you can never birth
but buy at the auction,
pawning acquired pride.

The tag of a sold scribe
is a shame
that the whole world must bear!

But, my womb is fertile still.
It shall voice more songs,
I shall yet birth
more children of dissent.
They shall face the world
with their heads held high
and sabre tongues.
They shall cut through the deceit
of the high and the mighty.
Decibel to decibel
they shall rise
to an earth shattering crescendo
and call the world
to a fiery rebellion!

As for the
pieces of my tormented mind,
they shall retrace themselves
back to me,
and redeem my name
from the clutches
of the brutish soul snatchers.

In that,
I shall taste my success,
an honourable victory.
My redemption
for eternity!

Lorca & I

If I had a heart-to-heart with Lorca someday,
this is perhaps what we would say...

Lorca in 'Before the Dawn' says-
"The keel of the moon
breaks through purple clouds,
and their quivers
fill with dew.
Ay, but like love,
the archers are blind."
To this I say-
"But like love,
lovers are blind,
they crash into each other
And then,
spark off to different galaxies...
never to meet again,
leaving the fire they raised,
unattended...
Never to glimpse at the marvels
they created together."

In 'The City that does not Sleep,' Lorca
contends-
"Nobody is sleeping
under the sky...
Nobody, nobody...
Nobody is sleeping.
If someone does close his eyes,
a whip, boys, a whip.
Let there be a landscape
of open eyes
and bitter wounds on fire.
No one is sleeping in this world,
no one, no one..."

To this I say–
"I preserve my brain in formalin,
for they burned the Library of Baghdad.
What would stop them
from gagging my words,
and start arson with the burning pages
of my poetry.
The City that never sleeps
glues its eyes to newer
and more novel deeds of brutality
and wishes away sleep...
lest nightmares catch them unawares
and my brain resurrects itself
to recall all the lost poetry."

Lorca, in the 'Gacela of the Dark Death'-
"I don't want to hear again,
that the dead do not lose blood.
that the putrid mouth goes on

asking for water.
I don't want to learn
of the tortures of the grass
nor of the moon with a serpent's mouth
that labours before dawn."
I say-
"I would close my book of fairytales,
See no evil... hear no evil... Do no evil...
But the holocaust is not a thing of the past,
Corpses pile up for mass graves
artillery still fresh for fire,
young lives still to be sacrificed...
The Red Sea is not red enough yet...
so let the bloodbath continue...
the Dead Sea is not dead enough...
So stifle my voice,
lest I begin to babble of
sunshine and butterflies...
of sugar and spice
and all that's nice."

But then, Lorca rues in the 'Gacela of
Unforeseen Love'-
"No one understood the perfume of
the dark magnolia of your womb.
Nobody knew that you tormented
a hummingbird of love, between your teeth."
I ask-
"Who says,
lovers are mild, delicate creatures?
They could put Lucifer to shame.
Turn you inside out,
carve the pounding heart from your chest

and offer it to their Gods...
like the Inca priests.
Tear away at your emotions,
like the crooked-toothed crocodiles
of the Nile.
and then coo into your ears, shamelessly,
'to love... is to bleed..."

Lorca observes
in his ode to his lover Salvador Dali
"Soldiers who know no wine
and penumbra
behead the sirens
on the seas of lead.
Night, black statue of prudence,
holds the moons round mirror
in her hand."

I cry-
"Hypocrites!
All you poets sitting here this day...
feigning to be benign lovers of peace!
What would you fill your platters of poetry with
if there was no pain, no violence, no war?
Own it! That you too
wait like vultures,
and prey upon tragedy, blood and gloom,
just like the crude soldiers you decry..
You hypocrites! You..."

Change

Woman! It is about time,
Change yourself!
Your silent, meek endurance
will really not help.
Woman! It is about time,
Change yourself!

Pushing you into fire,
Ram became Purushottam,
He revelled as the hero,
as you were thrown to harm.
Yank that mask of virtue
away from his face!
Woman! What have you done,
to deserve this disgrace!?

Why blindfold yourself Gandhari,
after a husband blind?
Why refuse to see,
and nurture an open mind?
Keep your eyes open
for you must open the world's eyes,

Woman! It is time you wake
and call womanhood to rise!

Who will come to save you
from ravage, rape and shame?
Your husband? Your God?
Your saviours, who never came!
Delude not yourself on stories
of gallantry and charms.
Women! Come together!
Rise up in arms!

Wrap not your tongue in fear and shame
utter the daring word!
Raise your voice against injustice
and let the noise be heard.
Step out under the open sky
the bells of change will chime!
Woman! Etch your history yourself,
upon the walls of time.

Let not the fetters of false virtue,
deter your forward march.
Renounce your fears, guilt and shame,
it's time to act harsh.
Tread upon the chest of the stifling
society in you must.
Woman! Be a rebel.
Break free from the past.

No one will arm you with weapons
like the Goddess of war.

Bathe in your own power, woman!
Brace yourself! Be sure!
It's time you stirred gunpowder
in your blood yourself.
Woman! Know your own strength,
You need no help!

Look into the mirror and promise,
to the woman you behold.
That you shall not just seek beauty,
but strive to be bold.
Seek not charity, solace or pity
you have your pride to redeem.
Let the world stand humbled in awe
invoke the power within.

Stand up woman! Wear your crown.
There's much more in store.
Live your life in honour and glory
It's worth dying for!

In Good Faith

Midas touched us today.
No, we did not turn into gold,
instead, his corrupt ambition
engulfed us with vengeance.
So, all us poets
sat together this day,
conspiring to kill poetry,
to extract gold
out of the very food
we seek to feed our souls with.

And why not?
When we have managed to
bottle water, can air,
sell the 'art of life'?!
Let's do it again!
In the name of 'Art',
at the altar of the Masters of Gold.

Let's behead poetry
and drink its blood
in cheap paper cups,

Whore it!
Sell sachets of chopped and brined verses
at the local tuck shop
and create
a brotherhood of innocent murderers-
A guild of the Merchants of Poetry!

And trust me,
we shall do all this,
in good faith!
Let our poetic liberty
crush poetry
under its grinding teeth
and mangle the words
into an uncouth yellow pulp.

Let us usher in
our own undoing,
bit by bit,
drop by drop!

Sprout

Long gone is the spring.
Mourning shrouds the earth.
The desolate sky offers no consolation
to the widow of the season past.

The brutal sun rises
like a heartless king,
flogging the earth
with its scorching rays.
Life crawls painfully
under the stifling dictates
of the incensed God.

The dry ears of the dead corn
stand defiant,
against the merciless sky
like a galley of brave soldiers.
The bubbly brook
gurgles no more,
an eerie silence
looms over the fields,
except for the relentless buzz
of the cicada

that refuse to accept
the harsh decree of fate.

Tossed and turned by the wind,
borne away from its tree,
a withered leaf drifts by,
spent of all its greens.
Wearing the brown of age and dust
it blows away,
out of sight.

But, from the cracking earth somewhere
sprouts a young seedling.
Struggling out of the unwieldy soil,
with an uncanny zest for life.
Pale, stunted
yet, stubbornly alive.

Alive!
With one desire burning in its heart,
to avenge the withered leaf
and the green field someday.
The cicada buzz on endlessly,
goading the seed, through all odds.
The brave corns
shall not die in vain!

A Fairy Tale Upside Down

What if my fairy tale
began at the tail?
Flowed upside down?
Began at the scene
where the handsome prince
kisses the fair maiden,
against the silhouette
of the great castle
with the towering turrets
raised into the starry sky?

Miracles would cease to happen.
The prince would drop the maiden
where she belonged.
The silver coach
would turn into a pumpkin.
The black fairy's magic
would fail miserably.
The maiden would turn into a baby
and the bored king and queen
would not know what to do...
because
the beginning never mattered much.

But then,
fairy tales never begin that way,
that is the politics of the fairy stories.
They never look back,
for, stark reality follows them
close at heels.
The skin shed by the fairies
are picked up by the rag-pickers
and the 'Happily everafter'
does not even figure in their
impoverished vocabulary.

Witching Hour

I wish,
I be a witch sometimes,
Brewing emotions
out of bloodied hearts,
honey and venom...
Conjuring dreams...
nightmares too...
The crystal ball rolls,
clouds over,
shows nothing,
but a blue haze.

The dark kohl in my eyes
keeps me awake.
I see, an unending seeing...
Hear, what no one hears...
Feel the dread of knowing all.
It is a curse, not a boon,
to perceive the beyond.
It kills the moment!
Leaves behind a nought
a darkness,
where I dwell.

But, I have my own world too.
Frog princes await the kiss,
Chameleons stare wide-eyed...
snakes, coiled in wicker casks
gather poison in their bites.
I have seen the asp
choking on its own spit.
Black pearls shine in
arachnid eyes,
as they crawl across
their silky webs
of treachery and deceit.

There is little hope
for the creatures of darkness.
But I set my raven free,
Go bird!
Follow your heart!
Taste freedom!
Never come back,
Leave!!

The poor broom
stands patiently beside the door,
awaiting the curtains
to come down...
for me to follow the raven
across the nimbus clouds
over the sullen moon...
beyond the dark night sky,
to meet the golden horizon
at the break of dawn.

Vanity

Locked in my own world again,
doing what I love best,
do best.
Oceans of stories
swirling around me
my characters... my people
holding me in a warm embrace.
Each speaking his own secret,
to reveal,
what shall surface as
yet another work of art.

Behold me!
Ye lesser mortals!
As I step into the shoes of God,
to create epics of my own
to conjure parallel worlds of alluring visions.
Create my own universe of
numerous galaxies
after my caprice
and breathe life into them!

Let my flight of fancy
carry me to the pinnacle of glory!
Let me breathe the rarified air
that only the glorious are entitled to.

Ah!
The Vanity! The Vanity!
I know,
there must be a plunge hereafter.
I shall yet rejoice the moment,
for glory, is addiction!
And I have been corrupted!!

So let my vanity
push me over to a glorious end,
for we must all die some day.
Then why not bargain
for a memorable death?

Animal

It hung from the high walls
of the manor house,
looking down with
wide, glassy eyes.
Long antlers, branched out,
into the murky shadows
looming under the high ceiling.

The taxidermist
had done a good job,
installed life
in a dead animal.
or at least,
the pretence of it.
But how could he return the innocence
the deer had lost,
when he was tricked to death?
The eyes, therefore,
stared down, with a ghastly still gaze,
You can't match life... in death.

There were life size busts
of fiery bisons,

curly horned rams too,
bringing the God Pan to mind
by a grotesque turn,
of twisted imagination.
Dead Gods,
hanging high upon the walls
of the houses
of proud, dead hunters.

Men... Foolish Men!
have always sought pride
in the number of births and deaths
they bring about.

Perhaps,
they deem it a signature
of their existence...
An existence,
that, with brutal whimsicalness,
brings about death and life.
The nonchalance,
giving great satisfaction
from the brazen show
of masculine virility.
Or perhaps,
it is the fear of death,
of being forgotten.

The blood line
and the line of blood
that they draw upon the earth,
brings about bastards
and the curse of dead animals

upon human kind.
Perhaps,
they find pleasure
in this dark game.
Flaunting,
this wicked trait of wildness...
Man, after all
is a vile animal!
And a loathsome one
to the core!

Four Seasons

Spring, springs to life,
sprouting shrivelled seeds
out of their deathlike hiatus.
The greens do begin to give
an illusion of harmony.
But soon a riot of colours follows.
They vie with each other,
jostle for space...
It is a battle for survival,
even at the peak of plentitude.

A cruel sun
mows down the children of green,
the ones that the spring had birthed.
Life perishes
in the raging summer.
The thorny cacti cling to life
defying the fatal decree of heaven
Gods do not
expend mercy on innocence.

Autumn, colours
a faraway land in blood,

the greens shall drown
in a crimson deluge.
Darkness descends early.
The fall, shall inexorably
ring in a blood bath.
Tread the woods warily,
lest the fallen rise again
and demand life once more.

In the land of auroras,
the cold hands of winter,
smother life
with grotesque calm.
A pall of serene death
descends quietly.
Blizzards of fine snow
powder the deceased.
Chandliers of frost
hang from limbs,
frozen in rigor mortis.

Thus pass
the seasons four,
to begin
all over again!
Indeed!
There is no justice
in the merciful God's
cruel world!

Beauty & Brain

My brilliance
shall outlive my breath,
for my ink is thicker
than my blood.

So lead me
to the slaughter house!
Guillotine my head!
Let the fools
laugh out aloud
as my head rolls
and my eyes glaze.

Let the inane
and the mundane rejoice!
Let there be a spark
in the tedious monotony
of their lives,
as my spilled brains
radiate the brilliance
of an eccentric dreamer.

Let the terror stricken see
what freedom and
fearlessness can birth.
What joy
in the consummation of
beauty and brain!

Without Background Music

Tragedy struck me
at the stroke of midnight yesterday.
But, what struck me most,
was the innocuous ruthlessness
of reality, thereafter!

Violins did not break out
in a dramatic chorus
of devastating strains...
The sky did not fall from its perch
creating a black hole
in its place.
The oceans did not surge
to engulf humanity
in my grief.
The wind
did not stop blowing,
choked by my pain.
Lightning
did not cleave the heaven open
to demand justice
against my ill fortune!

Nothing! Oh Nothing
stopped
because tragedy had befallen me!

The brilliant sun rose
all the same
on the rosy horizon.
The pigeons,
on my window sill,
would not stop preening!
A passerby
made a lewd gesture at me
as I sat benumbed
in the balcony
overlooking the street.
The deafening hum
of the noisy city
didn't stop
for a minute of silence
to mourn my loss!

What struck me most,
was the realization,
that the innocuous ruthlessness
of reality
is the highest drama of life!
That, how lonely we are
in our own
cooped-in devastation!
That,
tragedy sets in quietly,
without background music!

I Refuse

I refuse to be
a pigeon of peace,
cooing inane niceties
ad nauseum!
I demand justice
for all the atrocities
human kind has suffered.

I refuse to accept
that the blooming bud
wanted to blow himself up
for nothing!
I shudder to imagine
what it would have taken
to convince him
that death
is sweeter than life!
Who anointed his young body
with gunpowder
and handed him
the sceptre of hatred?

I refuse to forgive
the brutal rapists
who mauled
the tender body
of the innocent child!
I refuse! I refuse! I refuse!
to let the juvenile fiend go!
Let not yourself be fooled!
Let you not imagine that
the brutes are
far away!
They shall come
for you, for me...
They shall come,
for all of us!

I refuse to
let your God dictate
how I shall live!
None of your scriptures
impress me anymore!
Your Gods Lie!
Feign benevolence,
when all they really do is
to spew venom!
Your God is a reptile
that preys on your faith!
I pride myself
in my faithlessness!

I refuse to forget
the little child
lying face down,

on the shore
of the dead sea.
I refuse to believe
that it was the storm
that killed the boy!
He was a strange traveller,
going from nowhere
to nowhere!

I refuse to accept
that the hands that feed us
should crave for a morsel!
How carnivorous
can you vegans be?
Beefing up you coffers
of bankrupt piousness!
You shall not escape
the holocaust either!

I refuse to accept
that my dream is shattered!
It may have been
broken though.
Be warned,
That it shall resurrect itself!
Through the dreamless slumber
of the blind sheep,
my dream shall appear
victorious!

Be warned,
that Time, is upon us!

Nepal! We Cry for You!

The proud rock shed tears
of devastating avalanches.
It bowed its haughty head
and conceded a whole inch!
The day when the mountain crashed,
the bowels of the earth
sent tremors through its guts
and shook the giant from its sleep.
Who says,
the high and mighty can forever ignore
the unrest of the underdogs?

The men of science put it simply-
even a child would laugh
at their queer expression-
'A collision between two plates!'
But which child was left to laugh
when thousands lay dead?!
Nepal! We cry for you!

Shocked and aftershocked,
it trembled, not knowing
when the nightmare would end.

Nor did anyone know
when it would begin again!
It shook the very core of faith...
as it did the houses, temples and the city.
Trust was lost
upon the most trusted.
Mother earth had betrayed!
We came undone!
The Richter recorded the magnitude of
unkindness
when the earth gave away.
She spoke her language... and how!
Nepal! We cry for you!

We were not untouched,
though it was just a nudge.
The threat bypassed us
to befall you!
You bore the brunt,
flattened, cracked and broken,
a mangled little country!
Nepal! We cry for you!

A mere swing of mood perhaps
at the heart of the earth,
left countless dead,
under the unrelenting sky.
The jackals came hooting,
to prey on the flesh of humanity.
Even the Gods stood trembling
in their shattered temples
as helpless as the ordinary mortals...
we watched helpless too!
Nepal! We cry for you!

Silences were observed,
funds raised,
children at the school
wrote essays on the horrors
while the media minted money
...you went homeless,
hungry and helpless.
But trust us...
from the bottoms of our manicured hearts
Nepal! We cry for you!

www.ingramcontent.com/pod-product-compliance
Lightning Source LLC
Chambersburg PA
CBHW032109170626
46808CB00008B/2995